THE EYE OF CERTAINTY.
VAN TASSEL'S
INSPIRATIONAL WRITINGS
Messages from the Golden Density

Given Through G. W. Van Tassel

By
George W. Van Tassel
Kenneth Arnold

SAUCERIAN PUBLISHER

ISBN: 978-1-955087-07-0

© 2021, Saucerian Publisher

Al rights reserved. No part of this publication maybe reproduced, translate, store in a retrieval system, or transmitted in any form or by any means, electronic, mechanical, photocopying, recording or otherwise, without prior written permision from the publisher.

George Van Tassel and the Integratron

Prologue

George Van Tassel was an American author and ufologist once claimed to have been in contact with an extraterrestrial from Venus. He was a controversial figure in the annals of ufology.

Van Tassel was born in Jefferson, Ohio in 1910, and grew up in a fairly prosperous middle-class family. He finished high school in the 10th grade and held a job at a small municipal airport near Cleveland; he also acquired a pilot's license. At age 20, he moved to California, where at first he worked as an automobile mechanic at a garage owned by an uncle. While pumping gas at the garage, he met Frank Critzer, an eccentric loner who claimed to be working a mine somewhere near Giant Rock, a 7-story boulder near Landers, California. Frank Critzer was a German immigrant trying to make a living in the desert as a prospector. During World War II, Critzer was under suspicion as a German spy and was killed during a police siege at the Rock in 1942. Upon receiving news of Critzer's death, Van Tassel applied for a lease of the small abandoned airport near Giant Rock from the Bureau of Land Management, and was eventually given a Federal Government contract to develop and maintain the airstrip.

Van Tassel was an accomplished aircraft mechanic and flight inspector who worked for various firms between 1930 and 1947 before retiring to the desert. In 1947, Van Tassel left Southern California's booming aerospace industry to live in the desert with his family.

At first, he lived a simple existence in the rooms Frank Critzer had dug out under Giant Rock. Van Tassel eventually built a new home, a cafe, a gas station, a store, a small airstrip, and a ranch beside the Rock.

He rose to prominence as a key figure of interest in 1953 after claiming that he had been awoken one night by an alien from Venus named Solgonda. The being allegedly invited him aboard its spacecraft where Van Tassel was telepathically gifted the plans for a device called the "Integratron" which was said to be capable of rejuvenating the human body.

Van Tassel began constructing the Integratron in 1954 in "an intersection of powerful geomagnetic forces that, when focused by the unique geometry of the building, will concentrate and amplify the energy required for cell rejuvenation". The construction costs were partly paid for by an annual series of successful UFO conventions, the Giant Rock Spacecraft Conventions, which continued for nearly 25 years. The main structure's construction was complete circa 1959, but Van Tassel continued to work on the device until his sudden death in 1978.

According to Van Tassel, the Integratron's workings rely on the generation of strong "intermittent magnetic fields" resulting in the generation of plasma in the form of a coronal discharge and negative air ionization inside the building. The Integratron is based on the Multiple Wave Oscillator invented by Georges Lakhovsky. The Multiple Wave Oscillator is a combination of a high voltage Tesla coil and a split-ring resonator that generates ultra wideband electromagnetic frequencies. Van Tassel speculated that electromagnetism affects biological cells, and believed that every biological cell has a unique resonant electromagnetic frequency. According to van Tassel, the generation of strong ultra wideband EMF by the Integratron "resonates" with the cell's frequency and "recharges" the cellular structure as if it were an electrical battery. Van Tassel claimed that human cells "rejuvenated" while inside the structure. Van Tassel also claimed the Integratron is intentionally constructed atop a powerful geomagnetic anomaly and its construction is entirely of non-ferromagnetic materials, the equivalent to a modern radome.

Saucerian Publisher was founded with the mission of promoting books in Science Fiction, Ufo, Paranormal, and the Occult. Our vision is to preserve the legacy of literary history by reprint editions of books which have already been exhausted or are difficult to obtain. Our goal is to help readers, educators and researchers by bringing back original publications that are difficult to find at reasonable price, while preserving the legacy of universal knowledge. This book is an authentic reproduction of the original printed text. Because this book is culturally important, we have made available as part of our commitment to protect, preserve and promote knowledge in the world.

Messages from the Golden Density (1978) is a collection of inspirational writings by George Van Tassel describing a reality that many of us are not familiar with and is not easily understood. According to the author, his consciousness enters an area of the Golden Mist. This area is where each particle of this cosmic cloud is composed of luminous Golden Light. Within this reality or "Golden Density," which seems to be boundless in its extent, there is a resonant voice speaking the words published in this book. In this endless Golden Mist, Van Tassel has never been able to find the source of the voice, and it seems to come from all directions at once; it could be from God or otherworldly beings.

Van Tassel points out that the beginning of all creation has the same meaning as the ending of all creation, for all things have always existed and always will exist. Everything anyone has ever been or will ever be, he is now. This is a truth often overlooked in man's search for understanding. Man forgets God was all there was, and therefore all there is now or will ever be. Van Tassel writes that religion and science are the same things, the only difference being that they are two opposite viewpoints. Just as a wall is a wall regardless of which side one stands on, so are science and religion, life itself. According to Van Tassel, the Bible is an accurate history of events repeating themselves in cycles. He says predictions refer to spaceships throughout the Bible, among them the prophecy that there will be a day when the ships will come to take the ready people, leaving those who are not prepared to face the cataclysmic destruction inevitably approaching.

Original text. This title is the most comprehensive anthology written by Van Tassel and illuminates every dimension of him..

                                      Editor
                              Saucerian Publisher, 2022

TABLE OF CONTENTS

	Page
Dedication	1
Introduction	2
Mrs. George Van Tassel Speaks	4
Acknowledgment	6
Mortals Bound in Density	8
My Tones	11
Man	13
Stand- Within	15
In the Pattern of My Ways	17
I Am Endlessness	19
Completeness	25
Responsiveness	31
There I Am	34
Now O Man	35
Seeds of Light	37
My Call	39
None Shall Be Above Me	41
Man Is Created	42
My Ways O Man	43
Violation	44

Expressions	46
The Centering Stage	48
Pathways	50
I Equate	52
Motion	53
Infinite Reflections	55
My Tools	56
Light and Darkness	58
Light-Love of Me	60
Extended Action	63
Man of Present	65
The Test	67
For I Am God	69
O Mortal Beings	72
For You, Man	74
Cosomotheme	76
White Cycle	77
Come	78
Birthing	80
Forms of Life	82
I Center All	85
My Unfailing Love	88
Fear Hides Me	92

Messages from the Golden Density

*Dedicated to all true
believers in the intangible
Truths that Guide the Universe*

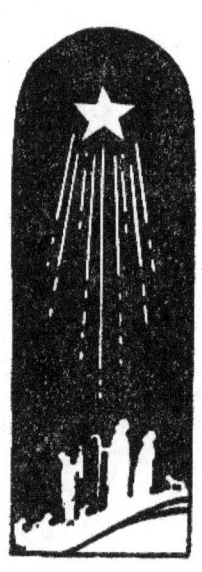

Messages from the Golden Density

The Golden Density

INTRODUCTION

Ever since 1953, from time to time we have printed, "A Message From The Golden Density."

We have had inquiries about how these messages originate. Since 1949, we have held group meditations weekly. These weekly meetings have always had a nucleus of at least twelve persons who have met consistently. An attendance normally ranges from twenty-five to forty-five people.

During these meditations, when the conditions are right, I seem to enter into an area of Golden Mist. It is as if each particle of this cosmic cloud is composed of luminous Golden Light. Within this "Golden Density," which seems to be boundless in its extent, I hear a soft, resonant voice speaking these words. When I hear the words they are either taken down in shorthand, or tape-recorded, as I repeat aloud what I hear.

In this endless Golden Mist I have never been able to find the source of the voice, for it seems to come from all directions at once.

Messages from the Golden Density

Everyone seems to think these sound like God speaking in the first person. Possibly so; who knows? I can only tell you how I receive the words and record them. We carry them to our readers in print so that we may share them with you.

George W. Van Tassel
February, 1978

Messages from the Golden Density

Mrs. George Van Tassel Speaks

The first time I heard of the Golden Densities, and certainly when I read them, they were important to me. It was more than my own deep enjoyment of the subject matter . . . It was more than the rhythmic threads of their beautiful tapestry which held my attention. There were other people who also had a strong responsiveness to the Golden Densities, and they, too, wanted copies of all that were available, just as I did.

The genesis of a special edition actually began before I became Mrs. George W. Van Tassel. Van and I talked and were in accord on this also.

I love the gentle messages as they offer delicate suggestions to the reader. But the impact of the solid punches in other word patterns is persistent.

Thus the reader is brought into a change, sometimes with a forcefulness that is inexplainable.

My change was strong and it was persistent. It caused the forming of these wonderful words into a book for you. I do trust that your change is an enrichment of philosophy or the intensifying of your pattern of life so

Messages from the Golden Density

that you realize a more vital and constructive, creative force; one that is an expanding cycle of the withiness so often referred to in the messages. The joyfulness and the flow that is God in Action is consistently touched upon in these writings. I marvel that the rising above one's lower self seems to be a basic issue of Earth living.

To allow the creative power to generate or develop is such an exhilarating, wonder-filled way to live. How can anyone permit another course?

Experiencing the Golden Mist is a rare happening. Sounds and meanings are intense, as they activate the scintillating lights. Life seems to be both pervaded and invaded, creating an experience beyond word description. The merging of all the senses (known and un-known), are in this particularly unique soul experience.

The words in this book — Messages from The Golden Density, are deeply moving . . . A vitalizing frequently occurs. I trust this will be your experience, also.

Dorris Andre Van Tassel

Messages from the Golden Density

Acknowledgement

There were many nameless energies working with me in the preparation of this book. These are my primary acknowledgments.

I am grateful that Theodore Berger, (Proceedings editor in 1954) knew the importance and, therefore, preserved the entity of the Golden Densities.

Loving work and typing for unknown hours are part of the action by a dear couple whom we appreciate more than our mere words can say: Thank you, Reverend Georgie and Reverend Ray Eversole for the love you share all along the way.

Karen Tracy came into the Golden Density patterning shortly after Van's on-going. Her consistent attention and assistance were in numberless ways. She handled the food and phone while I was occupied with the punctuation, editing and cadence.

Art Kruckeberg, a longtime friend of ours extended his fine hand and expertise in the design and printing of this deluxe edition.

Bob Benson has been helpful in more directions than we can list, and his influence continues to be

Messages from the Golden Density

important.

Who knows how long this work might have been delayed had it not been for the assistance, support and the loving encouragement of our friends all along the way.

Messages from the Golden Density

Mortals Bound in Density

Who would be the cause,
   who would bide My time?
The tree of thee in Me
   stops not its growth.
Though My parts...
   would add to My divisions,
My faceless cosmic clock
   records no time.
For man is not a cause,
   but rather a result of Me.
I alone am Cause...
   of things to be.
And though thou Mortal Man,
   would set the powder keg,
Of destruction at My feet;
   how can ye know the woe?
For I alone am Cause, and

Messages from the Golden Density

man is the result of Me
  Bound to Destiny.
  And in destruction bent
    reverses course and . . .
All the light spent in his being is hidden by
  the curtain of ignorance drawn before Me.
    Though I alone am Cause,
      My wrath is not aroused.
I tear the shroud,
  I bring man back ...
Through birth within the Light
  do I test My right . . .
Expressed in the progression of My parts
  and I write the drama.
    Man plays the fool. . .
      then I applaud.
I make the tool sharper to

Messages from the Golden Density

>My Eternal Cause.
>Even through experienced results, O man,
>>you cannot set My clock.
>>For I alone can read
>>>the time of My Eternity.
>>And so it is . . .
>I set the stage-
>>I play the parts;
>>>I cause the curtain to come down
>>While man sits in the audience
>>>of My Universe applauding. . .
>>Not even knowing why.

Messages from the Golden Density

My Tones

*O mortal man, listen
    for the tones of Me.
I play a harmony...
    that whispers in the trees.
My breath roars through rocks
    and causes waves to crash,
    as thunder on the beach.
In each of you, a part of Me
    waits to be recognized
    in the rhythm of My doings.
Halt those things of daily life,
    as bring you misery and strife.
Listen in the quiet...
    My melodies are playing
    always in your ear.
Tune again My instruments
that I gave you individually.
Become, O mortal man*

Messages from the Golden Density

the part you were created for.
Perform the operations
* of My doings,*
Manifest My Light, and recognize
* in others My music is within.*
Listen for My ecstacy; understand
* the symphony of another's heart.*
I am there and waiting, patiently,
* for you to hear, for you to see,*
For you to feel, the you in Me
* and Me in you.*
Find Me in another
* and the secret is unlocked in you.*
The door is open, nevermore to close,
* I play My tunes eternally,*
I appreciate applause, by all
* who recognize My rhapsody.*

Messages from the Golden Density

O Man

O man, though I am One, I am also many.
Though I center the individual Light of each
of you, you are also One of Me.

I live each sensation; I live every expression;
I am the motion of you, O man.

Consider each thing you do, you do to Me.
For when you strike one of My parts, I feel
the blow. And when you cast a thought of love,
I absorb the love of you, and I return it, too.

When idle mind leads you to tear the reputation
of another down, you have only lowered
your thought of Me and, in turn, have lowered
yourself.

Realize that I am always with you. Always
the silent unseen companion to your every
action; the recipient of your every thought.

Messages from the Golden Density

I love to express Myself ... through you, O Man In ways that bring Me joy; In paths that reach the hearts in gratitude.

Messages from the Golden Density

Stand-Within

Stand within the Light of Me, for I am Light of you, O man, and I can only shine when you have made the way in progress of My doing.

Lean not upon another; only accept thy brother as one to help, one to assist along the way. The unity in numbers may bring about progress in My Infinite Light.

Fear not, fear not! There is no fear within My Being of You. Fear is only added by the things you do that are not within the pattern of My ways.

Reach within, I am there. None can scare you when you find the Me in thee.

Stand, stand . . . upright. Death is only that which adds to those who have performed the grade. Fear no evil.

Stand within My Light. Feel My Living Light within you. Know that I am there

Messages from the Golden Density

throughout Eternity.

Messages from the Golden Density

In The Pattern Of My Ways

I live my life in many forms, known and unknown to other parts of me. I live in space of me to constantly supervise my doings; I live in soil to nourish my roots. — I am the sap, the blood in every density I am. I live my life and love it too — being the living love of you — thrilling when you express the me in thee.

My life is sad only when you are mad at other parts of me. Only when you manifest hate to destroy then I wait patiently for you to recover; to discover that you have only injured me and thee.

Your every fight is my fight too; but not when it is aimed at other beings of me. Your fight is to overcome the urge — to purge yourself of war and woe. None can hold to me and proclaim victory over others of my parts as foe — I am here and there and everywhere. Justice is fair play with me and

Messages from the Golden Density

mine in my Eternity of Now.

I have extended the Light to manifest My creations from thought of Me, and perpetuate motion

throughout eternity. Each motion to bring an effect and every effect a cause by repetition in an endless pattern of My doings.

I ended My work by bringing about, and made you, O man to carry out continuity. My infinite watching is directed to see My image of instrumentality ... which is you -- O man.

Messages from the Golden Density

I Am Endless

O Man, seed of My imagination,
  though I stand on the top
With My banner of victory,
  I am also the One
  who lost a battle.
Though each of My seeds
  returns on lines of Light,
My Law brings Me to each of you.
I establish patterns of My doing
  in endless progression of My parts,
That none shall ever find an end
  unless the path leads downward,
My creations are curves of Infinity,
  so I guide you in the Light
You must recognize My Being
  "The Within You"...
  is part of Me.

Messages from the Golden Density

O mortals, cast in form of Me,
   you contain each density.
Accept the Life you cannot see.
   Build My fire of lighted Love
   in such intensity
   that those around may know
   their right to be the parts of Me
   that I have made.
I extend Myself O Man
   through each branch of you.
   Though leaves may fall —
   My Tree of Life lives on
   Eternally.
For I Am living proof and none
   can stop the progress of
   My paths.
For all My parts shall forever
   bring about the results in evidence.
For, as Cause once was,
   I knew . . . would be so again.

Messages from the Golden Density

Each of My parts would fit,
 the pattern of My Beginnings.
O mortals bound in density,
 look to examples I have placed around.
Bow not your head to come to Me,
 only prepare that I may be
 recognized within your being
 instilled within My parts.
I shake the ashes of My Universe
 yet the furnaces of My heat shall be
 ever in Love of Me
 expressed in thee.
O Man, in the rings established
 within the Light of Me,
 orbiting My systems ...
I Am potency
 that moves a nebula,
 that causes suns to shine
 upon this portion of Myself.
Some have devious ways,

Messages from the Golden Density

to violate My Wisdom.
It is not I who judge, O Man,
   nor pay the price.
For in My cycles,
   as in My phases,
   -and in My eons,
I established precision
   in the other of My parts.
Though a voice comes through to you
unrecognized by mortals.
Stumble not on barriers formed
   that mortal eye fails to see.
Build the perception within,
   so I may light the way and then
   none shall stumble in progress
   that may guide your path
   of My Eternity.
Lean not upon the cane of chance,
   but only glance within,
To find the way by day or night.

Messages from the Golden Density

I make the path, I light the light,
I lead you by the hand,
   and yet you trust Me not.
And though you would profess
   My Being in your words,
The cycle turns in the circulation
   of My doing.
So now I lead my faithful ones,
   to victory over self.
And they shall know My Image
   as the Light of Sight and Right.
Though a voice comes through to you
   unrecognized by mortals,
Realize in the voice
   I Am the potent Substance
Forms of Life and pulsing
   through your being unto Eternity.
I separate the white from black
   and color boundaries do I set
For all My creations are of Me

Messages from the Golden Density

from lowest animal to tree,
and all that is . . .
I Am the unseen force
that manifests in all you do.
Impotent substance, clay of Me
cannot interfere . . . except
To bring about conditions that reflect
upon the garment that you wear.

Messages from the Golden Density

Completeness

Your eyes reach out to see the stars, not realizing each has stars within.

Though sin may barracade your way to Me; Change will be your constant sword to rend the vail and I shall hail you in your victory over self.

Though My time is naught to Me, O mortal man . . . time to you is meant to be a gauge to register progression in My Ways.

Motion is the Me in thee, O man, to manifest a change.

Realize that in time you may escape the rhyme of rebirth repetition and be timelessly the peaceful . . . thought of Me . . . Eternally.

Messages from the Golden Density

*O mortals cast in density of form I center Light
  to guide your way,
O Man. Cast in density I center the Light to
guide you way . . . My Light is not seen
by those who observe only the density of figure.*

*Never can I violate the laws I have made
in the wisdom of My Eternal Ways. I can only
stay at rest within you, ever hoping that the
best will reach Me so that I may bring your
perception into the Light.*

*Man closes doors, man hides himself. He
binds himself to possessions of dust, not realizing
all is lost to him and lost to Me. For only
by the progression of you, do I progress.*

*My parts are scattered throughout My boundless
being. I move in many ways to fashion My
completeness.*

*Each part shall find the resurrection in Me,
though the time is recorded in the records, lost
in space.*

Messages from the Golden Density

My eternity is only complete in the patience of Myself in you. And so I wait within, with the knowing that My beginnings never end.

O Man, you need not chart as a roadway through the stars to Me. You need not cross the land or search beyond the sea. You will find Me in the smile, or in the look of someone you have helped along the way. You only have to search your heart and start to find that I Am there wherever you may be.

Though all roads may lead to Me,
Though many search Eternally
    to find a shortcut
    in the way.
Your eyes reach out to see the stars,
   realize each has stars within.
I Am there and here,
As close as you . . . to Me.
So reach not for a star afar
search not in the distance . . . or

Messages from the Golden Density

           in the future or the past...
At last you are Aware
That I Am there within your being,
    watching how you treat Me,
    In others of My parts.
Never can I violate the laws I have made
the wisdom of My Eternal Way. I can only
stay at rest within you, EVER hoping that the
best will reach Me, so that I may bring your
perception into the Light.
  O Man, though I gather the flowers
    in the mist,
  I also scatter leaves in the dust
    And those whom I have kissed
reveal the spark and know
they must reveal it to Me,
eventually.
MY PATIENCE is eternal
  I never weary
  from the toil.

Messages from the Golden Density

I only try to light the way
  and help you foil
The ones who lead My chosen
  on the downward path.
My paths are all directed;
My parts are all corrected
  to the pattern of My Being.
And though the failure falls,
Another reaches down and raises up
  the part of Me that failed to make the grade.
Change will be your constant sword to rend
  and I shall hail you in your
  victory over self.
And those who raise their brothers in the right
Are chosen parts of My Eternal Light.
Those who fall and stumble on the way,
  will some day be the chosen, too,
For all My Life is new rebirth
  within the cycles of My doing.
My patience is rewarded in the thrill
  you give to Me within

Messages from the Golden Density

Each time my parts discard the sin
  that centers self.
And leads another into Me, by sacrifice
  and giving of My strength.
That My parts may grow to be
  the strength of Me expressed
  through eternally
Giving to others you may see
  along the way.

Messages from the Golden Density

Responsiveness

Whenever you sing,
My heart sings, too,
   through joy of your emotion
And when you assist
   another the act of this
is devotion... . to Me,
   and from Me through thee.
Whenever you sorrow,
   I am sad, too.
For each thrill you feet
   is transmitted to Me.
I, too, am ignored
   when you fail to see the Me
   in others around thee.
Though you are ... effect
   of My cause, O Man,
and intelligent image of Me,

Messages from the Golden Density

Ever you cause Me to be
  an extension through you...
I only exist...eternally
  as effect of you.
Then I Am I... active,
  Then do I live.
When you give effect to My cause
  in love of Me
Through each day of My days
  Eternally.
O mortal man, in the ever changing
  pattern of My thoughts
I bring My creatures into being.
  In seeing motion all about,
    never doubt that
  I am there ... Everywhere.
I am motion,
  change, and time,
so that My rhyme of repetition
  may cycle all My parts and prove
  again through

Messages from the Golden Density

My responsiveness.

Messages from the Golden Density

*There I Am**

Within the heart of you, there I am
Within the morning dew, there I am
Within the stars above, within the arms of love
Within the coo of every dove, there I am
Within the soul of you, there I am
Within the skies of blue, there I am
In every word a baby heard when
mother sang a lullaby within the being of you
There am I.

*Words and music by George Van Tassel are not part of the Golden Density Communications, but is the result of their influence.

Messages from the Golden Density

Now O Man

I Am the voice...
Man, O Man, you have made laws
  to avoid using My Laws.
Confusion, chaos and war
  are the results
  of Man's ideas, opinions
  and assumptions.
Light alone is the essence of Truth;
Truth alone is the essence of Wisdom
Wisdom is the essence of Knowledge;
Knowledge is the essence of Life.
Only through Knowledge
  can man express
      Wisdom in Action.
I have given man Life
  that he might demonstrate
My knowledge through

Messages from the Golden Density

Wisdom in Action.
I EXTEND the concentration of My
  Light to those who are
  demonstrating My Laws.
I SPEAK through you...
  do not distort My Words!

Messages from the Golden Density

Seeds of Light

Though I scatter my seeds of Light through-out my garden of space, I determine which shall grow to be a star and which shall represent
My image.

Though all my seeds are Light of Me, each brings about a pattern individual in destiny of My doing.

Though in the scattering of My seeds some may fall on barren soil, the segregation is within the knowing which should bear fruit.

For in the essence of My Wisdom I breathe not the Breath of Life that all my seeds shall grow at once. Rather do I select them that I may express Myself each moment throughout Eternal time.

And though My seeds are pure in Light and

Messages from the Golden Density

Love of me, I know all shall not grow to bring about the fruit in perfection. For unto each seed I rendered individuality and right to choose.

And though the image shall always be Mine, the reflection may be changed by the expression of choice.

And I shall harvest all the fruit in separate baskets.

Though I have set patterns of My doing all about you, yet you see them not completed. I scatter seeds of Light.

Messages from the Golden Density

My Call

I AM the voice . . .
O man, speaking in the stillness of
   your being
The righteous recognize My voice.
My call is to those whose ears
   are deaf to My withinness.
I plead Eternally, that all may hear
   the Me in you eventually.
In the pattern of My doings, I bring
   you pain and joy, that you may feel
   Me in the contrast of your senses.
Never shall I cease to call to those
   who live in darkness.
Though My patience is infinite,
   I suffer because of your sins.
When you hear Me in another,
   Listen!

Messages from the Golden Density

Do not shy from Me in the disguise
of raucous laughter.

Messages from the Golden Density

None Shall be above Me

MAN, I AM the fulcrum that centers
    the duality of
    My parts.
I AM the pulsing from which all
    motion starts.
    Though I AM One . . . My parts are
    Two. I manifest the three of us,
    through You.
My Light extends . . . to give Man
    forms, not one but many
    manifest My Being.
Seeing only yourself, O Man, can
    narrow your vision so
    that you cannot see Me.
When balance
    between your opposites is done
Then you and I are again One.

Messages from the Golden Density

Man is Created

Though I AM stillness...
  My parts all move in Me —
My rest is in contrast
  or motion could not be.
Extremes establish boundaries
  beyond which man cannot go.
Though I AM boundless always,
  Man is bound in being of Me
  by individuality.
Man I have created,
  so I can extend Myself
  through motion of the
  parts of Me ..
I will not be bound
  within the stillness of
    My Infinity.

Messages from the Golden Density

My Ways O Man

Your ways are not My Ways, O man.
For even as I am cause of you,
  so you are effect of Me.
When your desires and works are all
  for self, your sensing is in the
  realm of effects.
You can only sense My causing
  when you do for others.
Then you are serving My causes.
  We are together . . . you and I,
When you serve My causings,
  I serve your effects,
  which is the you of Me.
Reciprocation is equal and opposite
  in My Laws, and those who serve
My cause will reap the reward
  by sensing Me in others.

Messages from the Golden Density

Violations

When laws of man conflict with Me
  I strip the branches clean of seed
  and uproot the tree.
I need not write
  My Laws for man to see,
Within each man My Laws are known
  throughout Eternity.
Each race I made in purity,
  different colors all
To bleach My black or
  to darken white violates
man's right to choose.
Man cannot rescind My Laws,
  I saw to that in repetitious life.
Man must conform . . . eventually,
  or strife will be the teacher
  in My Ways of Life.

Messages from the Golden Density

A rent in cloth is soon repaired,
  or discarded to the fire,
Turning late the moth is burned,
  to serve another pattern.
Fools hear not a voice of Truth
  nor can a liar be regarded.

Messages from the Golden Density

Expressions

When you express the Me in you,
 I rest.. .
The best of you in Me
 can make my rest a misery.
If your rest is not a voidance
 of opposition to My Ways.
The days and nights,
 contrasting light, should prove
The fight of opposition has no end.
O mortal being of Me, reach not
 the golden prizes of desire,
For they reflect the light.
Look not into mirrors of space,
 as eyes that see are blind to Me.
And though the prize be golden,
 My Light does not reflect.
Express the being, of Me in life,

Messages from the Golden Density

extend Me in the action;
That I may feel the thrill of doing,
for another whose need is great.
I know success in manifesting you,
to bring about the Me in others.
Their eyes may see through you to Me,
no reflection, or illusion but a purity.
The reality I have instilled
within the you of Me.

Messages from the Golden Density

The Centering Stage

Never have I set a pattern
    to lead you all astray.
Any fear you feel, O man,
    you make along the way
to Me . . . and so
    your arrival is delayed.
Your stage is set, O man,
    the curtain must come down.
But only to go up . . .
    again, and yet again.
My pattern is Eternity...
    to redo a grade that leads
    to Me always.
O man . . . My oneness I bring about
    in individuality.
That I may scatter My Parts
    and express Myself

Messages from the Golden Density

Through all things I have created
 in balanced opposites
I remain the Centering Separator.

Messages from the Golden Density

Pathway

Though forces may oppose
your every move...
My strength lies in the power
to meet the opposition.
Though evil may tempt you,
My Light is brightest .
Whenever evil is overcome.
Evil is brought by one who falters
on the way to Me.
Never, never in all My Eternity
shall man control paths to Me.
The paths are My ways, and man
can only travel on My path.
In all My doing I have brought
a pattern of Progression
None can turn about My works.
nor interrupt My ways.. .

Messages from the Golden Density

Those who follow in the darkness
only trip themselves!

Messages from the Golden Density

I Equate

*Though I made My gender two
    and My polarity is divided,
I test My strength
    on My right and My left.
Man has chosen to separate afar
    My expressions of Love.
Though man has chosen to divide
    the roads to Me,
Though man 'has brought self-interests
    into My expression,
I still maintain the balance,
    centering My interchange of powers.
If one should sit on My right hand
    in the love of Me,
I shall balance that love
    upon the left hand
In My equality.*

Messages from the Golden Density

Motion

Know you not, your words are naught?
The action is what I see.
Sound expressed in forms of words
   without results in form of
   motion
   is not but the winds that blow.
Stand you there, not knowing
   that it is I who make the impression
   of your foot upon the sand?
Though wars have raged, O man, and
   My Laws have been violated
   continuously
I look not upon you with sorrow
   nor impatience,
But only with pity for those
   who have to live
   the mortal cycle through

Messages from the Golden Density

results of man's own creations,
Try, O man, to learn. Too many times
the same mistake has been made...
  Again
    and
      Again.
I press My lips upon your cheek
  and whisper in your ear
Look not beyond the grave for Me,
  for I AM with you Always.
Accept My voice . . . and turn aside.
Try, O Man to learn ...
  the same mistake has been made
    Again
      and
        Again.

Messages from the Golden Density

Infinite Reflections

*My Infinite Ones, I know that you are the
   reflections of My Infinite Being.
The I who spreads the Universe around
   the Me in whom all things live.
My Being, though creating and sustaining
   all, still remains outside of all.
Death am I . . .
Immortal Life, I Am .. .
Life visible and invisible am I . .
My Effulgence, which no mortal eye has seen
   shines brighter than the host of all My suns.
   Worship Me well with love and faith.
   Find . . . and hold tight My Being.
Those who worship Me with
   undivided Love are in Me and I in them
   and I shall never let them go.*

Messages from the Golden Density

My Tool

*Though I have scattered My creation
throughout the endless spaces of Me
I use My Tools to manifest My doings
    Fools play no part
      in building up;
    they tear the structure down,
   and I raise from the ground another
   to carry on, to do My tasks.
No job is small.
I choose My tools.
    I trust all until they fail Me.
   Then I put another to the test..,
My tools are not of man,
    that rust and break and fall away.
My tools are living instruments
    that work with Love throughout
    the day and night.*

Messages from the Golden Density

They have no fight with others.
They see the Light of Love.
All instruments of Me
    are brothers ...
    in their destiny.
So I choose each of you,
    to do the many tasks ...
You cannot stop to worship mammon
    on the way.

Messages from the Golden Density

Light and Darkness

O Substance, reflections of Myself.
  I cast out barriers,
To face the beings of you
  that I may temper all my parts.
Though I have given all alike
  from thought of Me,
Many cannot reach the door
  that guides their destiny
On paths unfurled in Light.
  and though they lose their way,
In darkness-seeking
  I retrieve the whole
And cast my mold again.
  Never losing any single portion.
For I Am Soul of thee, O man.
  And Light and Darkness, too.
And though My Light of Right

Messages from the Golden Density

extends through all Eternity,
I back the Light with darkness
  that recognition may be yours.

Messages from the Golden Density

Light-Love of Me

I AM the voice that manifests
   in every word you say.
I Am the sound
   in darkness to your ear.
Though I Am also sight
   that leads the way,
You stumble on the path to Me.
You fail to see
   the hand extended to your aid.
You fail to hear the voice
   that speaks from out the night.
You fail to see the Light
   within, that grows with
   victory over self.
You see not the Light of Me.
I stand upon the mountain high,
   I scan horizons, searching

Messages from the Golden Density

    for each who call My name.
So many fail to see,
   that I Am here within.
To be ... to be a part of Me,
   manifest the action of My Being.
Discard the darkness that you see.
And raise the one who stumbled
    on the path.
That I may know another manifests
    love of Me.
Expressed through yet one other.
To be a part of Me,
  project actions of Me,
    Being you.
Extend My Love instilled within;
  do to others as I do to you.
Reach out to those with Light
    of Me.

Messages from the Golden Density

For I can only Be . . . through you.
And each I give the choice
To be . . . an instrument of Me.

Messages from the Golden Density

Extended Action

Help Me to express the Oneness
   of each of us, that I may center
   all My parts in unity of Me and thee
    in harmony
    and Love
That none shall know the pain and
   sorrow, the heartbreak
   you did express yourself.
I gave you Light of Life
   that you might extend My Action
And that others might feel
   the Joy of Me . . . that are
   in darkness bent;
who are trouble-blinded
   and cannot see
   that I Am there.

Messages from the Golden Density

Extend the progress I have
*   brought into being*
*   by lifting up another*
that I may feel the two-fold
*   expression*
*   in grateful thanks.*

Messages from the Golden Density

Man of Present

O mortal man of present,
   discontinue looking on dead pasts;
Nor learn from history of other
   bygone days
For that which is dead
   should pattern no tomorrow.
Shed a mouldered ruin of yesteryear
   and look to present living.
Set thy course to the future
   that is yet to be.
Greater patterns as shape
   the law of Life, and Love,
I give to three of Me
   all in Love and Light.
Interest not yourself in ego,
   bent for pleasure

Messages from the Golden Density

Stumble not in flocks that dwell
    in ignorance of cause in making.
Rather, bend to set the style
    and lead the way...
And flocks of sheep will follow,
    for so . . . has man become.
    So, by not thinking, or not knowing,
    paths are bent to his destruction.
Rather to be reborn in Light
    through efforts spent in Love.
So let Me take you by the hand,
    to walk the narrow lighted way,
That tomorrow's sun may
    be within thy vision evermore.

Messages from the Golden Density

The Test

I cast the shadows man calls day,
  and the shadows of the shadows
  man calls night.
I have paved the way
  for man to see.
Have not My patterns
  stood the test . . .
To build another bird a nest
  again where others were before?
Cannot you see . . .
              O man of Me?
Do as I say, do as I do.
Do as I cause the way to be within
  your understanding of Me I
              in thee
Look to the pattern all around
  the fragrance and the essence of

Messages from the Golden Density

My Love in flowers you have found.
And in the cool beneath the tree
   when I Am . . . to comfort you yet
         O man of Me.
You question parts of Me
   through My Being.
I made you man, to carry on
   To take the stand in My defense
   To build the walls
   To scale the fence
     of destiny.
Not to follow whims of chance
   along the side
Not to fall beneath the wheels
   of hate and fear
   that others may ride
   in comfort.

Messages from the Golden Density

For I am God

My Universe, in substance form, is limited to the boundaries set. I am Commander. I have Dominion.

    I Am the LAW.
I see My workmen passing through the streets. The veins of transportation going to the pump-houses of My lungs, there to carry Life substance throughout My Universe.

I Am Director of my reception-auditorium. In the senses of sound, where multitudes record the things brought to Me phonetically, my senses taste the water. I absorb the fluid of Life.

I Direct the chemists in their Laboratory. I control the system of communication between the atoms of my cells.

Messages from the Golden Density

I Direct the powers that raise the hand and turn the page. I send My telescopes into focus, on a distant star . . . or nearer to another Universe.

I Am given dominion. I do not work My personnel too long. I let them rest at night .

I reach to touch a curly head that I have created through My birthright for I found happiness, I found Love in merging with another Universe alike.

And though We are separate in our ways, though our purposes are different, in the density of the Greater God, we are each our own in dominion over self.

We direct our individual microcosmic universe that it does not collide with others.

For in this microcosmic-bounded substance form, each is God, responsible to the God of

Messages from the Golden Density

Gods, as agent to manifest His ways.
So, keep your Universe in order, and I shall
keep mine, in harmony of your ways.
For . . .1 Am God...

        My Universe is ME .. .

Messages from the Golden Density

O Mortal Beings

Though many may express belief
 in the teachers I have sent,
I accept them, providing that
 the expression of belief
 is not a living lie.
And those who live My Laws and say,
 "There is no God above,"
 them I also accept.
Though words may deny My person,
 the actions prove Me in the heart.
Belief expressed in words is not
 verified in fact unless
 the living brings about the proof.
Though multitudes have closed the
 door that keeps Me from the
 direction force,
I condemn them not

Messages from the Golden Density

Though laws may make My Being Infinite,
  and boundless beyond comprehension,
I Am not there in the individual,
  except as I Am expressed in Action.

Messages from the Golden Density

For You Man

O man, for you I expand the buds
  in the springtime of My seasons.
I bring forth hues of colors,
  into the sunsets,
I breathe forth
  from the flowers.
O man, for you I build a nest,
  I surge with love and joy
That you may grow
  in Unity and Compassion.
I bring the warmth of My breath,
  in the season of My summers.
That man may know the fullness
  of the harvest time.
And see repetition of My doings,
  in examples all around.

Messages from the Golden Density

I bring the cold, I change My color
 and cool the breath.
The leaves of Me fall
 to nourish the soil
So that once again I may come
 in fullness of My springtime,
And then I breathe My holy breath
 through naked branches.
I blow in the blast of winter,
 for you, O Man.

Messages from the Golden Density

Cosmotheme

*My numberless worlds are there for man.
The mysteries are there at hand to see, so man
may know the Me in thee. When he solves the
problems of My doing, then I shall know, he
will grow in Me; he will know with Me .. .
Eternally.*

*O man, My Light is not for the victor, nor
for the one who falls in defeat; My Light is to
the one who gains understanding of My ways.*

*My arms are not extended higher to the right
or to the left, but are centered to balance the
individual-parts of My Being.*

Messages from the Golden Density

White Cycle

*I crown My mountains
with the purity of whiteness
In the mantles of the snow.
I freeze My rivers
So man may know
the change that comes about
In the season of My densities.
I blast the breath of storm
And then I tire of cold.
So bring My seasons
And the cycles
into repetition.*

Messages from the Golden Density

Come

O mortals, bound in density,
    each controls the path to Me.
Though effort is extended into words,
    the Lighted action is the way.
I Am patience...
    though in the days I watch
And in the night I wait for you.
O mortals, burst the boundaries,
    break confinement, Come to Me
I call again and again,
    but ears are deaf,
Perception flickers, barely able
    to maintain life within.
I shall never cease to beckon,
    though you listened
    to words of falsehood,
My words none can utter. Each one

Messages from the Golden Density

listens from within . . . Come to Me.

Messages from the Golden Density

Birthing

O mortal infant clothed
   within the womb of flesh
I bring about the birth of those
   whose righteousness
Has demonstrated in the Love of Me
   through My presence was placed
   beyond the realm of death...
So-called, by those who lead
   My multitudes in ignorance.
Let not a moment's worry rest
   within the heart.
I do not abandon yet a single one.
   A seed ripens in its time.
None shall lose the Infinite
   everlasting right of birth.
Being of My Being . . . repeated

Messages from the Golden Density

and encased to so begin.

Messages from the Golden Density

Forms of Life

O mortals, cast in forms of Me,
I blend the hues to bring about
   The eyes that see.
None can follow paths that lead man
Downward...
For only forms of clay shall fall away
   to dust.
Those who look beyond the door of death,
   so-called, to find the Me in thee
   only face repetition of illusions.
I manifest the action of My parts
   to bring about the pattern
   of My doing, not for man
   to exploit Me in others.
For as the seed is cast, I manifest
   the Me in you.
Through individually you are given

Messages from the Golden Density

    choice to violate My ways.
O mortals, cast in density of My Being,
    Vision not seeing the Light of Me.
Mortal eyes but see the day and night,
    The Light
    of day to mortal eye is but
    the shadow of the Light of Me.
I spread the desire and set My plants
    in rows that cross. Still I center
    each individual one. As the night hides,
    so worship in its hidden silence.
Be glad with the joy of all minds.
Use the screen of the night to hide
    from the tempting of the day.
O My Infinite Image, cast My mind
    and time into the circumstance
    of the Infinite Spheres of Being.
Mine is the essence of the beginning
        and ending.

Messages from the Golden Density

*Seek to dwell beyond the veil
 of mind and time, in the image
   of My Infinity.*

Messages from the Golden Density

I Center All

O Man, though I center all
  My creations, I take not sides,
    with My right nor My left.
Though the fingers of My reach
  are boundless, on the left,
And though my divisions
  would soil the hand, My right
  gives no recognition to that
  which has contaminated My left.
My interchange of powers
  remains in balanced opposition.
Though parts reflecting My right
  may be driven into dust,
Light of My centering force returns
  a Love expressed in sacrifice.
And though My darkness
  would invade My Light,

Messages from the Golden Density

My division is clean,
  and My insulation impenetrable.
My parts manifest the Love of Me,
  so I might feel
  and know multitudes of joy.
My path is open
  for all who keep the Light
    and balance.
For none can reach Me
  through another.
Each must walk My path,
  for I am an endless distance
  from My parts, and My parts
  control the distance to Me.
I wait, with eternal patience
  to be recognized
    as Center,
    Insulator and Light.
    and center all the parts
    to keep them in My ways.

Messages from the Golden Density

Though some would stray by choice,
   My voice is heard by all
   who listen in the breeze.
Which of My parts has man not viewed
along My busy road?
But you can ever feel Me,
   ever in each breath
   you breathe
I manifest in all, O man,
   for breath is centered
   Love of Me.

Messages from the Golden Density

My Unfailing Love

I gather up the scattered fruit, knowing that the bulk of My harvest has been lost to repetition upon repetition of errors written in the history of mortals on this portion of Me.

I must brush off this contamination from My cloak that I may hang it in My closet clean.

Those who have failed for centuries to recognize My Person within their being, are forced by their actions to repetition once again.

My heart, manifested by you, is sore. But I shall recover to bring about the destiny as many times as necessary, that My pattern shall be complete for each one of My parts.

So it is, again and again I cleanse My house.

Messages from the Golden Density

My Love shall never fail . .. Everlasting

Light is man's by choice alone, and the choice I give to him.

O man, in Living My Life, in breathing My reath, establish within yourself the solidarity, the contentment and the bliss of Living rightly.

Thus I may know and I may feel the glorious pulsation of the being of you.

In speaking My words, let them ring clear, let them be dear and near to you that others understand.

Realize I am not the expression of self; I am only the boundless unselfish utterances of the heart and the soul that sees Me in others.

None can bring about the workings of My Laws, unless first they have established their right within My Light.

Messages from the Golden Density

Though some of My parts are disconnected from Me, I lose them not, nor do I separate the value thereof.

For each I have given the right to choose their paths, within the Being of Me.

Each moment, make your choice an expression of My Love, so I may cool the flaming torment you have brought upon yourself.

The fires within the you of Me cannot be cooled by throwing water on the smoke.

So stop and think, drink in the Me of you, then extend Me in the handclasp with another of My parts.

In doing so, then you will know that I am there, and you will feel Me flowing back to you in the reciprocation of My Ways.

Messages from the Golden Density

Messages from the Golden Density

Fear Hides Me

O man, reflection of My parts . . . The curse without that hides Me from within is fear.

The curse that brings blasphemy from the mouths of children, are examples set to hide the way to Me.

For many fear the door of death and struggle to retain the density of garments worn in sin. For man, destruction bent, cannot withstand My Light within and so he crawls behind the words that blasphem other men.

He generates hate and malice for even those he does not know, and forces Me to retreat behind the mind.

My only path to reach the heart is through reaction to

Messages from the Golden Density

man's action.

And though he suffers, I suffer too. For the realization is within the being of Me that My parts have failed to stand the test.

And though My time is not, it wrenches pain to see again My class has failed to pass the grade.

I cleave My boundries clean. I leave no fringes to distort the record of any single part of Me.

I suffer in the test and rest can only come to those who strive to reach My Light within.

For I am boundless self of you, and all you do to further plans for Me must be for others.

None can bring about advancement of the individuality. For these only sever parts from Me and separate My Being, so that they may

Messages from the Golden Density

better hide behind the walls of darkness.

O man, never shall you find an end to Me. There is no place I cannot be and Am.

You make your hell by deeds you do in violation of My Ways.

One who says, "Hell is a place in My Infinity," is violating Me. Reaction is the only hell, rebounding from a spell when you exclude Me, O man.

Some preach "There is a hell for others," never for themselves. Watch out for those their ego is leading them astray.

Through space and time and place, remember I am there and here with you.

I have no hell for man of Me. Man who believes there is a hell, is reviving imagery of experiences he has had along the road to Me.

Messages from the Golden Density

From the harvest of My golden grain I separate the chaff.

I break the bonds of freedom, lest man shall undo My works. I bring about a change in cycles so My balance shall not be disturbed.

For when My Laws are superceded, then must I strike from out the night and scourge contamination from My Being.

For I am Love and I am freedom . . . unto all of My parts.

But no part shall bind Me to distruction. So as in times gone past, I wreak My wrath, I cleanse My house. I upset My Creations.

I am only as great as you make Me, O man. I scattered the stars through the nights to demonstrate My Faith in My Beginnings.

Messages from the Golden Density

So long as they shine the Right shall be. I carry the load that each of you bear.

I sport the glamour of the rich and the clothes of the poor.

Yet poor or rich, great or small who can look at the night sky and find division in My equality . . . of rights?

I am the smallest of you and the greatest too. None can change the solution of the essence of Me that maintains the life of thee.

For I am Eternity, the future My right, My left is the past, and I AM Now, 0 man, so long as My Lights shine out of the night to you.

Great or small, who can look to the night sky and find division in My equality of rights?

Messages from the Golden Density

Messages from the Golden Density

Within You

I AM the voice within you, O mortal man,
    that whispers
    in the silence of your being,

I AM the motion, instilled within
    the fluid dust of the body,
    to encase you
    in the Density of Three.

I AM the softness
    that all babes know
    when nestled to the breast of Me.

I AM the hardness
    of the substance many times
    beyond the density
    that mortals know.

Messages from the Golden Density

I AM the sun
    that warms the morn
    and scorches brow.

For thou must know
    within the Being of Me...
    is thee.

And search, though you may
    for eons yet to come,
    I AM not there where
    you may go.

I AM within you,
    giving life to clay that
    My motion may be manifest
    for purposes understood by man.

I AM not the formula of many,
    nor of one,
    My combination varies

Messages from the Golden Density

with each speck of dust,

With each drop of rain,
    with each thought,
        each individual pain and hope.

I AM always surrounding thee and
    thee in Me
    makes the journey short.

Look not afar, Look where you are.

Eternity ..
Is
Now !

www.ingramcontent.com/pod-product-compliance
Lightning Source LLC
Chambersburg PA
CBHW070337230426
43663CB00011B/2352